ANIMALS

Written by
Robin Robbins

Illustrated by
John Dunne, Martin Knowelden, Sean Milne and Sally Olding

Edited by
Caroline White

Designed by
Jo Digby

Picture research by
Helen Taylor

CONTENTS

The animal kingdom

Scientists have divided the animal kingdom into large groups called classes. Each class is made up of different animal species which are alike in important ways. This book introduces you to most of the classes, and helps you to understand how the animal kingdom is divided.

What is an animal?

Not all animals have fur. Many have bare skin, shells, feathers or their skeletons outside their bodies. Some have babies which grow inside them, while others lay eggs to make more animals of the same kind.

The animals on these pages are very different from each other, but there is one thing they all have in common. They eat their food by taking it inside their bodies. This is the simplest way to tell whether a living thing is really an animal or not.

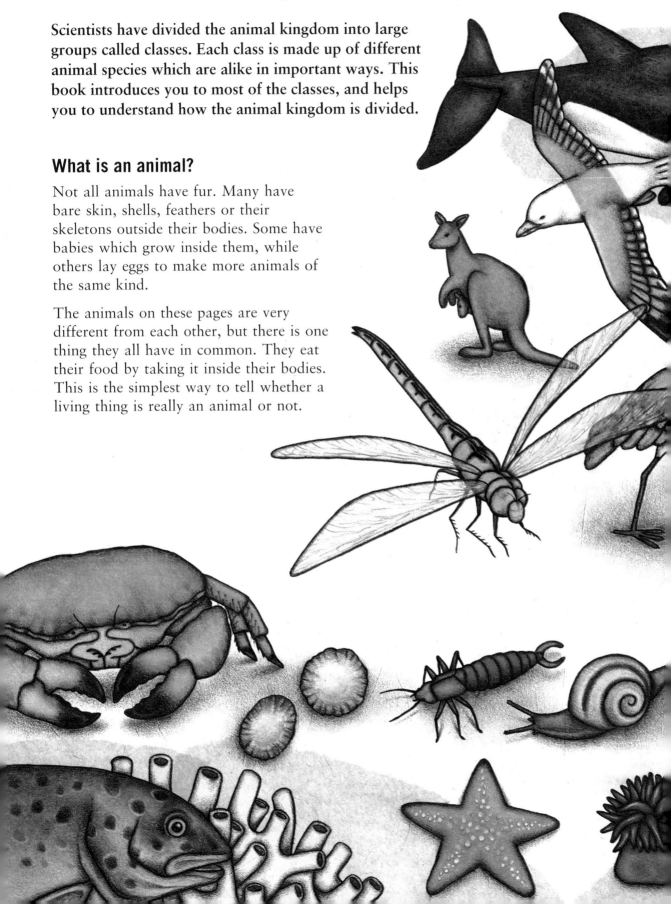

Worms

Worms may not seem the most exciting of animals. You may even think they all look rather similar! But there are three quite separate worm classes, which live very different lives.

Annelid worms

Annelids are worms whose bodies are divided up into rings called segments. They live in the sea, in ponds and on land. The kind we see most often are the earthworms that live in the soil.

Earthworms are very much alike, so you must look closely to spot small differences in shape and colour. They all have flat tails and a mouth underneath at the pointed end. Adult earthworms also have a 'saddle' where eggs are made.

If you run a finger along the underside of a worm, you can feel lots of pairs of bristles. These are used to grip the ground as the worm moves along. Amazingly the worm moves by pushing the liquid inside its body from the back end to the front and back again. This causes its body to stretch forward and then bunch up as it crawls along. The bristles grip the ground at one end while the other end changes shape.

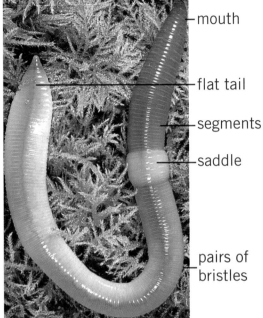

mouth

flat tail

segments

saddle

pairs of bristles

Earthworm

You sometimes see gulls marching on the spot on wet fields or sand. Worms sense the movement, which probably feels like rain, and up they wriggle to become food for the gull! On a damp day, try trampling for worms yourself. Test to find the most successful worm-charming place.

Earthworms are very important to gardeners and farmers. Their burrows let air and water into the soil, and they pull dead leaves down into the ground to eat. This helps to keep the soil mixed, while the worms' body waste adds to the goodness of the soil.

Many birds hunt for worms in the grass.

Nematode worms

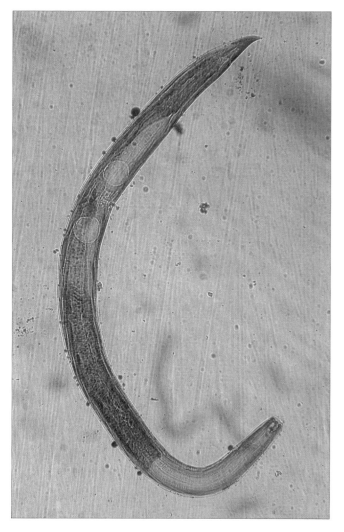

You will need a microscope to see most of these tiny worms. Nematodes are not related to earthworms and their bodies are not divided up into segments. There are probably more nematodes in the world than any other animal, with about 90 000 in one rotten apple and millions in every square metre of soil. Some nematodes are parasites, living and getting their food from inside another living thing. Indeed most plants and animals have nematodes living inside them.

Tiny nematodes can be found among rotting plants.

Flatworms

Flatworms live only in damp or watery places. Their bodies do not have segments, and they either eat other small creatures or live as parasites inside bigger animals. If you go pond dipping, you are sure to see flatworms oozing along in your catch tray.

There are several different kinds of flatworms.

Millipedes and centipedes

You will have to look carefully to spot the main difference between a millipede and a centipede. They both have bodies divided up into segments and lots of legs. But if you look closely at a millipede, you will see that it has two pairs of legs to each segment. The centipede has only one pair.

Millipedes and centipedes prefer to live in damp places, so look for them under rotting wood or big stones. Those found in this kind of habitat will have rather flat bodies, with legs spread out on either side. Other kinds live in holes in the ground. Can you guess what shape their bodies and legs might be?

The millipede's legs move in a wave.

When collecting millipedes and centipedes to study, put each one in a separate jar with some wet moss, because they will die if they dry out. You must remember to return them to their habitats as soon as you have finished looking at them.

Centipedes can move much more quickly than millipedes.

Use a magnifying lens to compare heads. The millipede has short antennae, which bend down to touch and feel the ground as it walks. Not all millipedes have eyes, and even those that do cannot see particularly well.

The centipede has longer antennae. It uses them to feel things as it hunts for small creatures to eat. To stun its prey, the centipede uses the poisonous pincers that curve round its head.

British centipedes are too small to hurt people, but in tropical countries there are some very big species which can give humans a painful bite.

All millipedes are plant-eating animals, so not even the big tropical ones will bite you. But for protection, many millipedes release nasty-tasting chemicals when they are touched. This does not always work, and birds and other animals may still eat them.

Millipede

Centipede

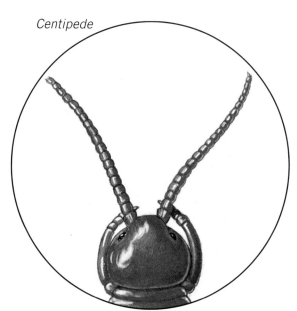

Mind-boggler

Did you know that centipedes can make good mothers? Some kinds lay their eggs in tiny underground 'caves'. They wrap themselves round the eggs and then lick them to keep them clean.

This centipede is protecting her eggs in an underground 'cave'.

What is an insect?

There are more insects in the world than all the other animals put together. Scientists already know more than a million species, and new ones are being discovered every day. But the lives of common insects still hold secrets that anyone can explore in a park or a garden.

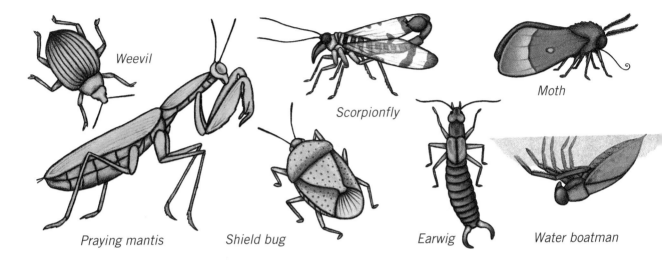

Weevil

Scorpionfly

Moth

Praying mantis

Shield bug

Earwig

Water boatman

The class of insects includes some of the most beautiful and interesting animals that you can imagine. Each insect is built to the same basic plan. Their bodies are divided into three parts: the head, thorax and abdomen. All adults have six jointed legs, while some of the young do not have legs at all. Insects have no skeleton inside, but they do have a hard outer skin called an exoskeleton. Almost all insects have one or two pairs of wings, although not all of them bother to fly!

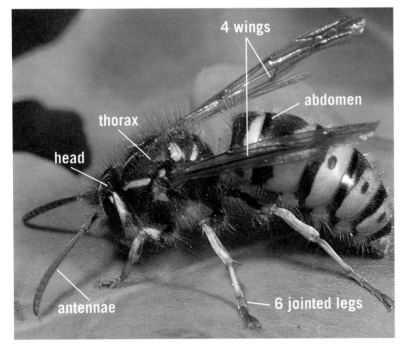

4 wings

abdomen

thorax

head

antennae

6 jointed legs

Common wasp

Looking closer

If you find a dead insect, a magnifying lens will help you to discover how it once lived. For clues about the food it ate, look at the mouthparts.

Butterflies and moths have a spiral 'drinking straw' called a proboscis to drink nectar from flowers.

Bugs spike plants and other animals with their sharp beaks and suck out their juices.

Flies spit on their food to dissolve it, then lap it up with their flat stubby tongues.

 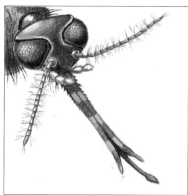 

Now look at the insect's two large eyes. These are made up of hundreds of tiny eyes, each seeing a slightly different picture all round the insect's head. The result is rather blurry, but just try to creep up on a dragonfly if you want to see how well it works!

Between the two large eyes you will find three smaller ones. Although these do not work very well, they can tell light from darkness.

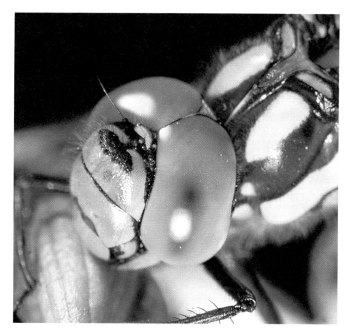

Can you see this dragonfly's eyes?

Metamorphosis

Young insects do not usually look at all like their parents. They may even eat different foods and live in different habitats. A great change must take place before they become adults. This change is called metamorphosis.

Insects such as ladybirds have four stages to their metamorphosis. The young insects are called larvae.

① The female ladybird lays her yellow eggs in little groups under a leaf.

② About a week later, the larvae climb from the eggs and begin to eat the aphids. As each larva feeds and grows, its skin becomes too tight and splits. There is a new skin underneath.

③ The skin splits for the last time, and underneath is the pupa. Although it looks very still, a wonderful change is taking place inside. The body turns almost completely to liquid and a new ladybird is made.

④ When the ladybird bursts out of the pupa, it is yellow and has no spots. But it will soon look just like its parents, and its metamorphosis will be complete.

The metamorphosis of a ladybird

Other insects have only three stages to their metamorphosis, because they have no pupa. The young of this group are called nymphs. They look rather like adults without wings, although you can see wing buds on the thorax.

male

empty skin

When it is fully grown, the nymph climbs up a plant stem and out of the water. Its skin splits for the last time and a new damselfly with crumpled wings emerges. Its wings soon unfold, and it swoops away to hunt for its first insect meal.

female

The male damselfly has claspers at the end of his body to hold the female during mating and egg-laying. He supports her while she dips her abdomen into the water to lay her eggs in the stem of a water plant.

folded mask

The damselfly nymph hatches from the egg and breathes through the three gills on its tail. Under its head is a folded mask which it can shoot out to grab its prey. As the nymph grows, its skin splits several times. Each time it splits, its wing buds grow a little bigger.

The metamorphosis of a damselfly

How insects live

Some insects live together and share the work of running the community. They include ants, termites and some kinds of bees and wasps. We call these 'social insects'.

Living together

There are three kinds of ant in the black ants' nest.

Worker ants just work all day! These female ants nurse the young and dig new tunnels. They soon die, but there are always new worker ants to replace them.

Male ants do not work. On a hot summer day they and the new queens swarm out and take a mating flight. Once they have mated, the males die.

When the queen has mated, she scrapes her wings off against something hard and finds a place for a new nest. She then rests until the Spring, when she will lay her eggs and nurse the first young ants. The new worker ants will grow up to take over all the duties of the nest, while the queen spends the rest of her life just laying eggs.

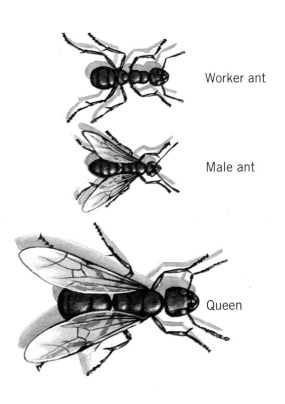

Worker ant

Male ant

Queen

These worker ants are looking after the larvae. Close by is an unmated queen.

Keeping safe

Many animals enjoy eating juicy insects. But insects have wonderful ways to keep themselves safe.

They surprise

The click beetle pretends to be dead, then suddenly clicks into a somersault, shocking its predator into dropping it.

The click beetle can be found in most hedgerows.

They hide

The grasshopper's green-and-brown colour means it can hide in the grass. Even if its chirp gives it away, the grasshopper can use its long back legs to spring out of reach.

Butterflies hide by folding their wings to the camouflaged undersides. To attract a mate, they simply open them out and display their beautiful colours.

The grasshopper is camouflaged in the grass.

They hurt

Some insects bite or sting, while others are prickly to eat. Although one insect may die when a young predator first tries to eat it, its death will protect other insects of the same kind.

They cheat

Animals know that wasps can sting. This harmless hover-fly has yellow-and-black stripes so that birds will leave it alone.

They warn

Ladybirds taste horrible! Their bright colours remind predators of an earlier, unpleasant meal.

Adult hover-flies feed from flowers.

In spite of this, millions of insects are eaten every day. But, of course, millions of eggs are laid by their parents to replace them.

Arachnids

Spiders, harvestmen, scorpions, ticks, mites and horseshoe crabs all belong to the class of arachnids. Arachnids are predators with biting fangs, an exoskeleton and eight legs. In most cases, their bodies are in two parts. They have a head and thorax joined into one and an abdomen.

Spiders

There are over six hundred different species of spider in Britain. Although they all spin silk, not all of them make webs to catch their food.

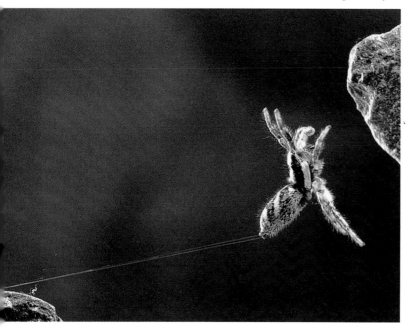

The little zebra spider hunts for food on a warm sunny wall or rockery. It uses its silk to make a safety line to stop itself from falling. The zebra spider stalks small insects, ending the hunt by jumping suddenly on its prey. Very good eyesight is needed for this, so the spider has eight eyes, including two extra-big ones at the front.

The black-and-white zebra spider belongs to a group known as jumping spiders.

Harvestmen

Harvestmen may look like spiders but they are not closely related and cannot spin silk. Their bodies have only one part and their eyes are perched on top. The harvestman traps its prey with its legs. It crushes it down and then bites off small pieces with a pair of pincers at the front of its body.

Look out for harvestmen in long grass and around stones.

Other arachnids

It is easy to find tiny water mites swimming along in the pond. Water mites are carnivorous animals and hunt for other small creatures to eat. They pierce them with their fangs before sucking out the insides.

There are over two hundred different kinds of water mites in Britain. They are very small, but a magnifier will show you how beautifully patterned they are.

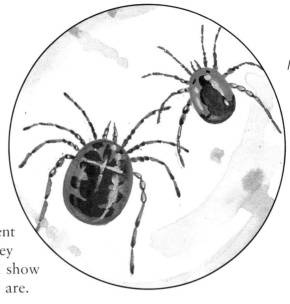

Most water mites are brightly coloured.

The pseudoscorpion eats land-living mites which it finds among rotting leaves. It looks like a miniature version of the scorpion found in hot countries, but it has no stinging tail.

The pseudoscorpion is less than 5 mm long.

Spot the difference

Make careful sketches of spiders' webs found on grass, bushes, buildings and walls. Each type of spider spins its own special web. With practice, you can decide who made the web without even seeing the spider!

Many webs have sticky strands to trap the spider's prey.

Crustaceans

Crustaceans have hard outer shells, which are usually jointed so the animals can move easily. It isn't always possible to see that their bodies are divided into three parts. They have two pairs of feelers, and in most cases ten legs. The front legs of lobsters and crabs have evolved into pincers. Almost all crustaceans live in water.

2 pairs of feelers

hard shell

legs

pincers

American lobster

Woodlice

Woodlice are perhaps the easiest crustaceans to study. You can find them under any damp stone in a park or garden. They will often be huddled up together or pushed into cracks in logs or between stones. They do this to stop too much air from getting around their bodies, because they will die if they get too dry.

Crustacean shells are not stretchy, so a crustacean must shed its old tight shell as it grows bigger. Underneath is a new, larger shell. Sometimes you find a woodlouse that is half white and half grey. It has already shed one half of its shell, and the other white piece will soon drop off.

This woodlouse is shedding its old white shell.

Like many water-living crustaceans, such as the prawn in the picture below, female woodlice carry their eggs and pale young under their bodies.

Barnacles cement themselves to the rocks and never travel again.

Mind-boggler

Seaside barnacles are crustaceans which are hanging upside-down! As larvae they swim in the sea, but later they fasten themselves onto the rocks, where they stay for the rest of their lives. Their plated shells are the part you see when the tide is out. But once under water, their legs come out from between the plates and wave about to collect their microscopic food.

Molluscs

Molluscs are animals with soft bodies. They include slugs, snails, mussels, whelks and squids. Molluscs have a head, a strong foot and a mantle. The mantle is a kind of soft bag that covers all or part of the body.

Some molluscs are only as big as a pinhead, while the biggest ones are more than 5 metres long! Most have a shell, although often this is hidden inside or is very small. Bivalve molluscs live in water and have two shells hinged together.

In the garden

Because slugs do not have a shell, either inside or out, they have no way to protect themselves from drying out and must always stay in damp places.

You can collect different slug species with a soft paintbrush. Put the slugs in a container with wet leaves while you study them with a magnifying lens. Their skins have beautiful colours and patterns, and you may enjoy painting a slug portrait gallery!

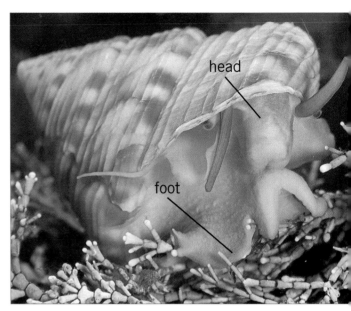

Painted topshells live in the sea.

Slugs can be sorted into two main groups. Keeled slugs are ridged along the back, like the bottom of a boat, while round-backed slugs have no ridge. Both these groups feed on plants.

You might be lucky enough to find one of a third group, the carnivorous slugs. Their narrow heads let them follow earthworms into their burrows, where they eat them. Carnivorous slugs have tiny shells at the tips of their tails.

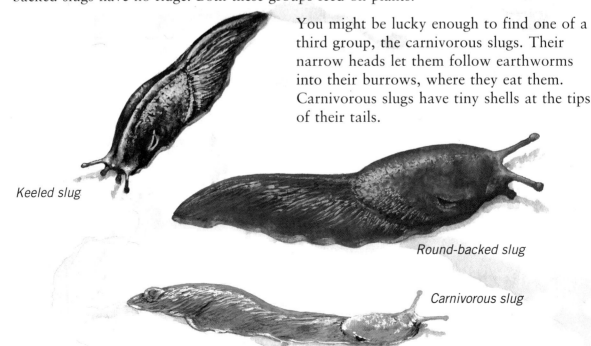

Keeled slug

Round-backed slug

Carnivorous slug

On the beach

In rock pools, winkles and limpets graze a trail through the seaweeds on the rocks. When the tide goes out, each limpet returns to the safety of a made-to-measure dent, which it scrapes in the rock with the help of its shell.

Carnivorous whelks eat other marine molluscs by boring holes through their shells. They particularly like bivalve molluscs, such as the tellins which live just below the surface of the sand.

These carnivorous dog whelks eat dead sea animals as well as molluscs.

The octopus has suckers on its tentacles. These help it to cling tightly to the rocks.

Mind-boggler

The octopus is a mollusc too! Its strong foot has evolved into a set of eight tentacles, which it uses to catch its prey. The octopus has no shell, but it can see well and has a good brain.

Fish

There are fish in the seas, rivers and ponds all over the world. Although we speak of 'fish' as if they are all closely related, there are three quite different groups.

Jawless fish, such as the lamprey, have toothed suckers instead of jaws. They use the suckers to fasten themselves onto other fish to feed.

This lamprey has fastened itself onto a shark and is sucking out its blood. .

Fish with skeletons of cartilage, which is softer than bone, include the sharks, rays, dogfish and skates. They have no flaps over their gills, and their scales have rough edges like teeth. Their tail fins are not symmetrical.

Smooth scales help the roach to swim easily through the water.

Fish with bony skeletons make up the largest group, with more than twenty thousand different kinds. Most have smooth scales and flaps over their gills. Their tails are symmetrical.

The fish in your tank

Aquarium fish soon learn to come to one corner of the tank every day if you always feed them in that spot. Choose the nearest corner so you can observe and sketch their adaptations to a watery life.

🐟 Watch a fish taking water into its mouth and gulping hard. This squeezes the water over the gills and out through the gill covers. As the water goes through the fish's body, oxygen is taken into the blood.

water gulped in here . . .   . . . and pushed out here

How a fish breathes

🐟 Compare the body of a fish to that of a submarine. This special streamlined shape allows for easy movement in the water. See how the scales overlap each other smoothly from front to back. This helps to reduce friction.

🐟 Watch the powerful tail acting as a propeller, while the fish's body flexes from side to side to help it along.

🐟 Check how the fish steers itself by moving its paired fins one at a time, like oars. Note that the dorsal fin flattens out as the fish speeds up, and is held high to keep it balanced when the fish is still.

🐟 Find the lateral line. This picks up vibrations to tell the fish that something is moving in the water nearby.

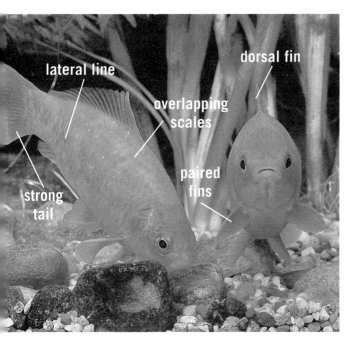

lateral line

dorsal fin

overlapping scales

strong tail

paired fins

Goldfish search for food at the bottom of garden ponds.

Strange fish

Not all fish have the same streamlined shape. They may swim upright or lie flat on their sides, and there are even some kinds which can come out of the water!

Sea horse

The sea horse breaks all the rules. It swims upright, so it isn't streamlined like other fish, and its dorsal fin, not its tail, moves it along.

The sea horse is a camouflage magician and can change colour in seconds. It can also grow whispy pieces of skin when it needs them to help it hide in the seaweed.

Last but not least, female sea horses lay their eggs in a pouch in the male's body. It is he who looks after the eggs, until the babies are ready to come out.

Sea horses live mainly in tropical countries, but their relatives, the pipefish, are found around the coasts of Britain.

The sea horse keeps in one place by curling its tail round weeds and rocks.

European eel

The European eel can wriggle over the dewy Autumn grass to find a river to take it to the sea. It swims down the river and moves into salt water as it enters the Atlantic Ocean. The eel's journey finally takes it to the Sargasso Sea, where it breeds and then dies. Its eggs hatch and the young drift back across the ocean to grow up in the ponds and rivers of Europe. When they are old enough, they too will make this long, last journey.

The European eel is a fish out of water!

Deep-sea angler fish

This deep-sea angler fish lives in almost total darkness. But on its head it grows a 'fishing line', complete with a glowing light. Smaller fish are attracted to the light and are quickly gobbled up.

Deep-sea angler fish live only in the deepest oceans.

Plaice

The plaice, like other flatfish, starts life the same shape as ordinary fish. But it isn't long before one eye moves to the other side of its head, so that it has two eyes on the same side. The plaice then spends most of its time lying on the bottom of the sea with both eyes looking upward, and with its fins looking rather like a fringe round its body. The upper side of the fish changes colour to match the sand and gravel on which it lies. When it swims from one place to another, it takes only a couple of minutes to match its new resting place.

Flatfish, such as the plaice, live close to the bottom of the sea.

Amphibians

Amphibian is a word that means 'on both sides of life'. The name was given because most amphibians start their lives as eggs in water, and then hatch into tadpoles with gills for breathing. But when they are adult, amphibians can come out of the water and onto the land, where they breathe air through their lungs. They can also blot up oxygen through their damp bare skins. By doing this, some amphibians can stay underwater for a long time.

There are three groups of amphibians in the world: frogs and toads; newts and salamanders; and caecilians.

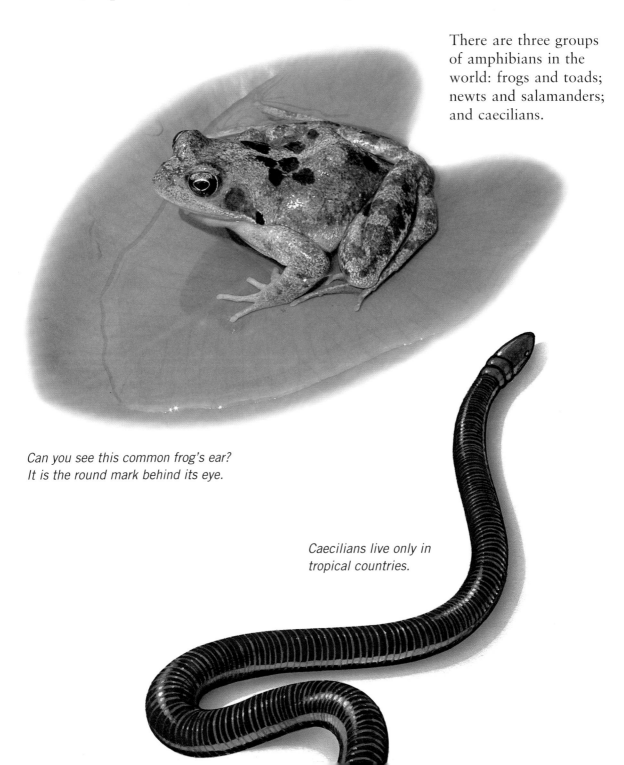

Can you see this common frog's ear? It is the round mark behind its eye.

Caecilians live only in tropical countries.

The common frog

In March you might go to a pond at dusk and hear male common frogs splashing about and calling to the females. At this time of year the male has a special rough pad on each hand to help him hold his slippery mate while she lays her spawn and he fertilizes it.

Frogspawn is laid in shallow water. At first it looks like a clump of black dots, which sink to the bottom of the pond. Soon the jelly protecting each dot swells in the water and the spawn floats up to the surface.

About a week later, the dots change shape and turn into tadpoles. The tadpoles have a frill of gills on both sides of their heads. A flap of skin will later grow over these and hide them, and the tadpoles will begin to eat other small creatures, dead or alive.

The froglet's back legs grow slowly, finally bending outwards like those of an adult frog. Its front legs grow inside the body and pop out from the gill covers when they are ready. About twelve weeks from the time the spawn was laid, the tail disappears and the tadpole's metamorphosis is complete.

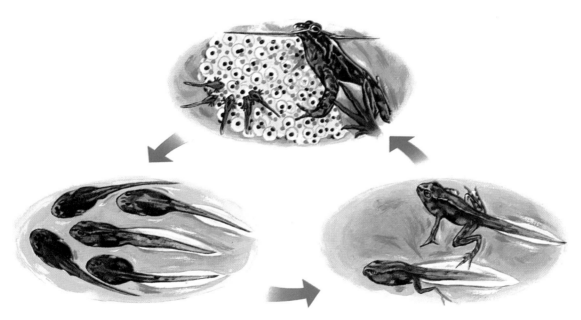

Life cycle of the common frog

Newcomers to Britain

In the past amphibians from other countries have been set free to live in Britain's countryside. They include the edible frog and the marsh frog. But please do not buy the exciting bullfrog tadpoles from North America which some pet shops sell!

Adult bullfrogs do not make easy pets, and it is now against the law to release any animal from abroad into the wild. This is because they sometimes compete with British plants and animals for food and habitats.

British toads and newts

Can you tell toads from frogs? British toads have a rougher, dryer skin than frogs. They move differently too. The common toad crawls along, with an occasional lumpy hop, while the rare natterjack toad scampers about in its heathland home.

Toads

In Spring, toads wake from their winter hibernation and crawl back to their home ponds to mate. The eggs are laid in two rows inside a long string of jelly, which the female twists around water plants. Common toad tadpoles are almost black, but natterjack tadpoles usually have a white patch under their chin.

Common toad

Natterjack spawn is laid in shallow water in sandy places.

Newts

There are three species of newt in Britain: the common newt, the palmate newt and the great crested newt. All three belong to the salamander family. Newts look rather like lizards in shape, but their skins are soft and damp and they move fairly slowly on land. Like frogs and toads, they spend a lot of time out of the water hunting for small creatures to eat.

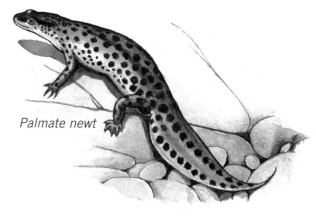

Palmate newt

Great crested newt

The palmate newt is about 7.5 cm long.

The common newt is about 8.5 cm long.

The great crested newt is about 15 cm long.

Male newts dance in front of the females to attract a mate, fanning their smell towards them with their tails. After mating, the female carefully wraps each egg up in the folded leaf of a pond plant. Newt tadpoles grow their front legs first. Their frill of gills can be seen until they become adults.

The male common newt has a spotted skin. He performs a mating dance in front of the female.

Hibernation

All British amphibians hibernate in winter. Newts often hide together under stones or logs in quite large numbers. Toads and newts hibernate on land, but male frogs will often spend the winter buried in the mud at the bottom of a pond, taking in oxygen through their special skins.

Amphibians around the world

Not all amphibians live in ponds or near water. From rainforests to grassy plains, there are amphibians living in different habitats all over the world. Some even bury themselves under the sand in the desert, and can wait years for the rain to come!

Common green tree frog

In Australia people often encourage the common green tree frog to live in their homes as a family friend. Like other tree frogs, they have sucker toes to help them climb.

With these sucker toes, the common green tree frog can climb up windows!

Cane toad

The huge cane toad was introduced to Australia from South America, because farmers thought it would eat insect pests. As the cane toad has no predators in Australia, there are now too many of them, eating useful creatures as well as plant pests. The poisons in a cane toad's skin are so strong that they can kill a dog.

The cane toad will eat most small creatures.

Strawberry poison-dart frog

The strawberry poison-dart frog lives in South America. It uses bromeliad plants as a nursery to look after its young. Bromeliads grow among the branches of rainforest trees, catching rainwater in the special cups made by their leaves. The female frog puts each of its tadpoles in one of these cups. Every few days she comes back to the bromeliad and lays an extra egg in the water for the tadpole to eat.

Poisons from the skin of the strawberry poison-dart frog are used by rainforest people on the tips of their hunting darts.

The colourful skin of the fire salamander warns other animals that it is poisonous.

Fire salamander

The fire salamander lives in Western and Central Europe. During the day it hides in logs and other damp places to keep its skin moist. In olden times, people sometimes saw it coming out from their burning log fires. They called it the fire salamander because they thought it had been born from the flames.

Caecilians

Caecilians are the third group of amphibians. There are many different kinds, but they can only be found in tropical countries. They have no eyes or legs and either live in water or burrow in dead leaves under rainforest trees. It isn't surprising that they are rarely seen!

Reptiles

Reptiles are sometimes called 'cold-blooded' animals. This means that their body temperature is close to the temperature around them. If they need to be warmer, they have to bask in the sunshine. To get cooler, they must hide in the shade.

Reptiles lay their eggs on land. The young hatch out of their papery shells as small versions of their parents.

Reptile skin is covered with rough, dry scales. The scales on the underside of a reptile's body are larger than the ones on its back. Some kinds also have bony shells.

The reptile family has lived on earth for over two hundred million years. There are about five thousand different species alive today. They can be divided into three main groups: tortoises and turtles; crocodiles and alligators; and snakes and lizards.

Sea turtles bury their eggs in the sand at night.

Tortoises and turtles

Tortoises and turtles have upper and lower shells to protect their bodies. They have hard beak-like mouths and no teeth. Although sea turtles live in water, they must come ashore to lay and bury their eggs. Many eggs and young turtles are taken by predators at this time.

Crocodiles and alligators

Crocodiles and alligators have many teeth, and their skin is covered with big hard scales. They lie flat and almost invisible in the water, watching for their prey with only their eyes and nostrils above the surface.

Snakes and lizards

The pit viper gives a poisonous bite to its prey.

Most snakes and lizards live on land. Their sensitive forked tongues can taste the wind to detect their prey. Some snake species have pits under their eyes which sense the warmth of an animal's body. This tells the snake that food is near.

Although a snake has no legs, it almost 'walks' on its ribs. The ribs are attached in a special way to help the snake grip the ground.

Tuatara

The tuatara is a reptile, but it does not fit into any of these three groups. It is a strange lizard-like animal from New Zealand. Its name comes from the Maori language and means 'spine on the back'.

Tuatara

Mind-boggler

The female American alligator sweeps together a nest of plants and mud with her body and tail. She then lays her eggs and watches over them to keep them safe. If the eggs are laid in a part of the nest where the temperature is lower than 30 °C, only females will hatch. If the temperature is more than 34 °C, only males will hatch. When they hatch, she gently carries the young alligators to the water in her mouth.

American alligator with one of her young

British snakes and lizards

You need to be lucky to see a snake or lizard in Britain. They are shy of human beings and will creep away when they sense the vibrations from your footsteps. Snakes and lizards are also hard to spot because their skins are camouflaged to match the places where they live.

Snakes

The adder is Britain's only poisonous snake. Very few people have died from its bite, and it will not harm you if you leave it alone. You may see male adders fighting for females on a dry sunny bank in Spring.

The stronger of these two fighting adders will mate with the female.

Grass snakes often grow to over a metre long. They prefer damp places and can be seen swimming in ponds, where they hunt for frogs and fish. Although the grass snake is harmless, it can leave a bad smell on your skin if you handle it.

Grass snake

The smooth snake lives only in a few places in southern England. It is especially rare because most of the sandy places where it lives have been destroyed to make way for farming or building.

Smooth snake

Sand lizard

Common lizard

Slow worm

Lizards

The sand lizard, like the smooth snake, lives on sand dunes and heathland. It is very rare indeed, because of threats to its habitats.

The common lizard lives in warm dry places throughout Britain. It is the only reptile that lives in Ireland. Unlike most other reptiles, its eggs hatch while still inside the female's body, and the lizards are born alive.

Although the slow worm has no legs, it is still a lizard! It can often be found in country gardens, and especially likes to feed on slugs in warm compost heaps.

Hibernation

When reptiles become very cold, they cannot move quickly to hunt or escape danger. British reptiles hibernate from October to around February to avoid cold weather and shortages of animal prey. Sand lizards dig a burrow for themselves. Other snakes and lizards find a ready-made hole, perhaps under a tree root. While they are hibernating, their body temperature drops and their heart and breathing rate slows down. However, on bright winter days they sometimes wake up to bask in the sunshine.

What is a bird?

From penguins to swallows, from vultures to parrots, there are over nine thousand bird species living in the world today. Although each species is different, they all have certain things in common. They all have feathers, wings and the scaly legs of their reptile ancestors. They also all lay eggs and are warm-blooded. This means that their temperature is controlled by their own body and not by the weather.

The world's largest bird is the ostrich. It measures about 2.5 metres high and lays an egg weighing 1.35 kilograms. Although it cannot fly, the ostrich can run at 48 kilometres per hour, and will fight and kick at any predator that can catch up with it.

The ostrich has huge feet to stop it sinking in the sand.

The Cuban bee hummingbird spends most of the day drinking nectar from flowers.

The smallest bird is the Cuban bee hummingbird, which weighs about as much as six paperclips. Its eggs are less than a centimetre long and are laid in a nest made of spider's webs. It can fly extremely fast, both forwards and backwards, and feeds mainly on high-energy nectar from flowers.

Feathers and flying

Most birds are wonderful flying machines. They have streamlined bodies, wings and keen eyesight. Their bones and beaks are hollow for lightness, and they even have special air-sacs leading from their lungs to hold extra air.

Feathers are shaped like long scales. A magnifying lens will show you that they are more complicated than they look! Each feather is made up of smaller sections, all zipped together by tiny hooks. If the sections are accidentally pulled apart, the bird can stroke them together again by running them through its beak. This is called preening.

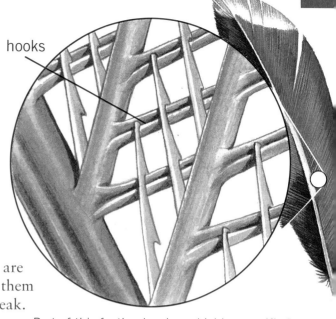

hooks

Part of this feather has been highly magnified to show how it hooks together.

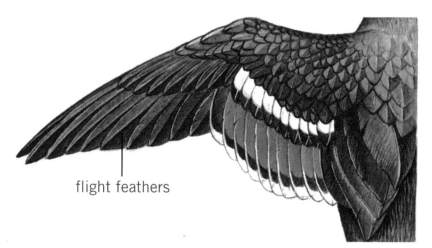

flight feathers

Birds have long stiff flight feathers at the tips of their wings. These push the air down as the bird flies, then open out to let air flow through them as the wings are lifted again.

Watch birds carefully to see how they fly.

Body feathers are waterproof and overlap so that water runs off them when it rains. Under the body feathers are fluffy down feathers for warmth. When a bird puffs its feathers up in cold weather, it is really wrapped in its own built-in quilt!

The robin puffs up its feathers to protect itself from the cold.

Bird life cycles

Most birds mate and lay their eggs in Spring. The male attracts the female by offering food or finding a good nesting place, or by performing a special dance called a 'display'.

The male then hops onto the hen's back and sends a liquid full of sperm from his body into the hole under her tail. Some sperm must swim into the egg cells inside her for chicks to begin to grow. A few days after mating, the eggs are ready to be laid.

Great crested grebes perform a mating display.

Chicks from ground nests can run about and feed themselves almost as soon as they hatch, although they still need an adult to guard them.

Chicks from nests in trees and buildings are blind and naked when they hatch. Bluetit parents can bring around five hundred caterpillars to their chicks each day for about seventeen days. Even after the chicks can fly, their parents carry on feeding them for several days, until they are able to hunt for themselves.

This lapwing has made a hole in the ground and laid her camouflaged eggs there.

Adaptations

The shape, appearance and behaviour of animals show how they have adapted to live successfully in their habitats.

The turnstone lives in a beach habitat. Its black-and-white feathers camouflage it against the pebbles. It uses its specially strong bill to turn over stones to find tiny animals to eat.

Turnstones can open mussels with their strong bills.

In open fields it is easy to watch the skylark singing as it hovers high in the sky. But you will not easily spot its nest on the ground, because the skylark's behaviour is adapted to deceive you. It will land quite a long way away from its nest, and then run secretly through the grass stems to reach it.

Ducks are just made for water! Their webbed feet help them to swim, and although they have no teeth, their bills have rough edges for holding wet, slippery food. Ducks also have an extra eyelid, which is clear. This allows them to see underwater. They search for food by tipping upside-down with their tails in the air.

Male ducks are called drakes. Their bright colours attract female ducks.

Migration

It is hard for British birds to find food in winter, although many species manage well on seeds, berries, molluscs and worms. Because insects usually die or hibernate in cold weather, most insect-eating birds take a long flight to a warmer country to find food. This is called migration.

Swallows meet for their long journey south.

Before migration begins, the birds eat as much as they can to store up extra energy in their body fat. Some even double their weight! Then they flock together and set off on their long journey.

Birds find their way over hundreds of kilometres using the sun and the stars. Young birds sometimes migrate later than their parents, but they still know how to find their way.

There are migration flights in all directions. Not all of these journeys are long, but they are all very dangerous and many birds die. Those which survive will return home to lay their eggs in Spring.

Mind-boggler

The Arctic tern makes the longest migration journey of all. Its main food is small fish, but as the Arctic winter draws in, the daylight hunting hours get shorter and shorter. So it flies across the world to the Antarctic. The journey there and back again is about sixty thousand kilometres!

Narrow wings and a trailing tail help the Arctic tern on its long, swift journey across the world.

Watching garden birds

You can help the birds in your garden by offering them food, especially in winter. Birds with short stubby beaks are seed-eaters. They enjoy wet brown bread and other foods made with grains. Those with needle-sharp bills are insect-eaters. They prefer cheese or meat. Experiment with different foods to see which birds prefer which foods. Soon the birds will become quite tame, and you can watch them carefully to find out about bird behaviour!

The chaffinch has a short stubby beak to help it crack seeds.

Bluetits cling to the thinnest twigs as they search for tiny insects. In winter they eat nuts and seeds, sometimes while hanging upside-down.

Noisy gangs of starlings chase each other and squabble over scraps of food. They love to have squawking, splashing parties in the bird-bath!

A male blackbird guards his own part of the garden, threatening other blackbirds which come into his territory. They fight, flying up into the air beak to beak.

Mammals

A mammal is an animal that feeds its young on milk made by the mother's body. Usually, but not always, the babies grow inside the mother. Mammals are warm-blooded animals. Most have four limbs and either hair or fur.

Egg-laying mammals

Egg-laying mammals, such as the echidna and duck-billed platypus, are often called 'primitive mammals'. Their soft-shelled eggs and the way their shoulder bones are joined show that they have evolved from the reptiles.

The duck-billed platypus is very rare and lives only in Australia. Its eggs are laid in a burrow in the bank of a stream. The female curls round the eggs to keep them warm. When they hatch, she feeds the young animals on milk from special glands in her body, although she has no teats.

The duck-billed platypus has webbed feet for swimming in rivers.

Pouched mammals

Over fifty million years ago the lands of South America, Antarctica and Australia were all joined together in one huge country. This was the home of pouched mammals, such as the kangaroos and koalas. Then these lands floated apart. The pouched mammals died out in cold Antarctica, and only a few now live in South America. But in Australia and its surrounding islands, they continue to live and thrive!

A newly-born kangaroo is as short as your thumb. Although it is blind and naked, it still manages to crawl through its mother's fur to the safety of her pouch. Inside the pouch is a teat, where the baby can feed until its fur grows and its eyes open.

Kangaroo and joey

This tiny red creature in its mother's pouch will soon grow into the bright-eyed furry creature above.

A baby elephant is safe under its mother's body.

Placental mammals

This is the largest group of mammals, and includes human beings. The babies of placental mammals grow inside the mother. Some of the oxygen she breathes and the food she eats is passed to the baby dissolved in her blood. Although most placental mammals are helpless when they are born, some can walk within a few hours of birth. But even these still need their mother's care and are fed on milk.

There are around four thousand species of placental mammals scattered all over the world. This book can tell you about only a few of them!

Mammals worldwide

Mammals live all over the world and have adapted to many different habitats. Because they are warm-blooded, their temperature usually stays the same, whether they are panting in the heat or fluffing up their fur in the cold. Some mammals hibernate in winter to survive the cold. Their temperature then drops and their heartbeat slows down.

In the oceans

Whales are perfectly adapted to a life at sea. Their front legs have evolved into strong flippers for swimming. Even their young are born in the water and can swim at once. Their bodies are streamlined and almost fish-shaped, although the tail moves up and down and not from side to side. They have a few bristly hairs, but it is the thick layer of fat under the skin which keeps them warm.

The whale's nostrils are at the top of the head. This allows it to breathe easily when it comes up to the surface. Some kinds of whales can stay underwater for as long as an hour.

The killer whale has teeth and feeds on animals such as seals and penguins.

One group of whales has teeth and feeds on fish and other sea creatures. Dolphins and killer whales belong to this group. Another group, the baleen whales, have a kind of strainer in their mouths instead of teeth. They sieve small creatures, called krill, from the water to eat. This group includes the blue whale, which is the largest animal on earth. The blue whale can measure up to 30 metres long!

The blue whale does not have teeth and feeds on krill.

In the South American rainforests

The three-toed sloth is so closely adapted to tree-top life that it could survive nowhere else. Its claws have evolved into long hooks which cling to the branches as it hangs underneath them. Even its fur grows downwards, in the opposite direction to other animals' coats. In the rainy season, the sloth looks green because tiny plants grow among its hairs.

The three-toed sloth moves slowly. This is because it only eats leaves, and there's no rush to find leaves in a rainforest! It comes to the ground just once a week, to leave its droppings.

A baby sloth travels through the trees clinging to its mother's fur.

The howler monkey has solved another difficult rainforest problem. The trees here are so thick that monkey families cannot see each other through the leaves and branches. So the howler monkey has developed a call that can be heard over 3 kilometres away. The call warns other families to keep their distance. It is so like a jaguar's roar that early explorers were terrified when they heard it!

The howler monkey's throat acts as a natural loudspeaker.

From African plains to farmyard fields

On the plains of Africa survival often depends on mammals living and working together in groups. While lions work together to catch gazelles to eat, the gazelles work together to look out for danger!

On the plains of Africa

Working as a team, sand-coloured female lions chase the plains animals to see which is the slowest and weakest. Once the prey has been chosen, the lionesses hunt without mercy, sometimes driving the animal into an ambush. When they finally catch their prey, they hold it by the nose or throat until it suffocates. The male lions, which are too heavy to hunt well, then push the females aside and eat first.

Herds of gazelles graze the tough grasses, grinding them with their strong back teeth. Their camouflaged coats match the scorched grassland where they live. While they eat, the gazelles scan the plains for predators. Dozens of eyes working together have a better chance of spotting danger. If a chase does begin, they will make zigzag leaps into the air to confuse their pursuers.

Lions hunt zebras and springbuk antelope on the plains of Namibia, Africa.

On the farm

Thousands of years ago, human beings tamed some kinds of plains mammals for use on farms and in their homes. In the eighteenth century, British farmers began carefully choosing which farm animals to mate with one another to produce the best animals for meat, milk or wool. In this way, special breeds of farm animals gradually came into being. They included Jersey cows, Hereford cattle and Cotswold, Leicester and Lincoln sheep.

Hereford cattle were known for their excellent meat and gentle ways.

Jersey cows give rich, creamy milk.

The Lincoln Longwool was prized for its soft wool, which was made into clothes and fabrics.

Charolais bull from France

It is not always easy to see these old breeds on farms today, because British animals are now cross-bred with those from other countries. Charolais cattle have been brought to Britain from France. They add their own special qualities to the old breeds, as they grow more quickly than British cattle and produce leaner meat.

Always, everywhere, some mammals are just kept as special friends.

Mammals and food-webs

There are many mammals in Britain's cool green woods. During the day you can watch squirrels scurrying about, or perhaps disturb a tiny shrew and be surprised at the loudness of its angry chatter! But most of the woodland mammals are nocturnal and come out only at night. They live very secret lives.

Each kind of mammal has its favourite foods. Woodmice, dormice, bank voles and fallow deer mostly eat plants. Bats, moles, shrews and hedgehogs prefer insects or other invertebrates (animals without backbones). Stoats and weasels eat other mammals, while foxes and badgers eat both plants and animals. You can join all the plants and animals in any habitat into a pattern of 'who eats what'. This is called a food-web.

Sometimes food-webs get damaged by natural disasters or by human interference. Stop and think what would happen to the woodland food-web below if the trees were cleared to make way for new houses. What would the plant-eaters do? If the plant-eaters all disappeared, what would happen to the meat-eaters?

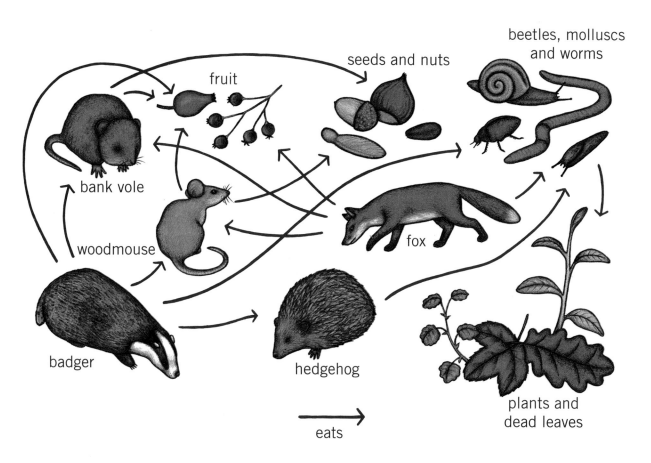

Who eats what in this woodland food-web?

All over the world

In deserts, oceans, rainforests, grassy plains and all other habitats throughout the world, there are food-webs linking together every living thing. People are part of these food-webs, suffering just as much as any other animal or plant if the webs get damaged. But unlike other animals, human beings can decide to help the world's wildlife. They can try not to damage its food-webs and habitats. If you would like to help the animal world, why not write to the clubs below to find out how to join? Please remember to enclose a large stamped addressed envelope.

WATCH,
Royal Society for
Nature Conservation,
The Green,
Witham Park,
Waterside South,
Lincoln LN5 7JR

The Young
Ornithologists' Club,
Royal Society for the
Protection of Birds,
The Lodge,
Sandy,
Beds SG19 2DL

Mute swans nesting in a polluted canal

Children clearing the riverbed of pollution

Take care of the wonderful animal kingdom. It is yours to share and to care.

For Calum and Malaika, with love

Published by BBC Educational Publishing, a division of BBC Education,
BBC White City, 201 Wood Lane, London W12 7TS
First published 1995
© Robin Robbins/BBC Education 1995
The moral right of the author has been asserted.

Paperback ISBN: 0 563 35539 5
Hardback ISBN: 0 563 39784 5

Colour reproduction by Daylight Colour Art
Printed in Great Britain by BPC Paulton Books Limited

Photo credits
Ardea **pp. 5** (John Clegg), **6 bottom** (Ian Beames), **17** (John Mason), **36
top** (Jack A Bailey), **45 top**; Bruce Colman Ltd **pp. 7, 9, 13 top and
bottom, 18, 19 bottom, 21, 22, 24, 28 top, 32, 34 top, 41 top and
bottom, 44, 45 bottom**; NHPA **pp. 8, 14, 30, 37, 38 top, 47**; Oxford
Scientific Films **pp. 4, 6, 13 middle, 16, 19 top, 28 bottom, 29, 31 top
and middle, 34 bottom, 35, 36 bottom, 38 bottom, 40, 41 middle, 43**;
Planet Earth Pictures **pp. 12, 23, 26, 31 bottom**; Zefa Pictures **p. 42**
Front cover: Telegraph Colour Library (**main picture**) *common British
frog in duckweed*; Bruce Colman Ltd and Telegraph Colour Library
(**bottom right**) *seven-spot ladybirds*

Illustrations
© John Dunne 1995 (pages 10, 11, 12, 24 and 25), © Martin Knowelden
1995 (pages 15, 18, 32, 33 and 39), © Sean Milne 1995 (pages 5, 7, 9, 17,
20, 21, 22, 23, 26, 27, 35 and 42), © Sally Olding 1995 (pages 2, 3, 4, 8,
37, 45 and 46)